HEALTHY LIVING

HEALTHY LIVING

Simple Steps to a Vibrant Life

B. VINCENT

QuantumQuill Press

CONTENTS

CHAPTER 1

Introduction

Rebekah Eliz teaches readers how to understand their body's direction to better health and how to bring their body into a state of balance through a simple, three-part "clean/feast/restore" approach that supports the body's innate ability to repair itself. In her book "Healthy Living: Simple Steps to a Vibrant Life," readers are provided with the much-needed information, inspiration, and motivation to help ensure that each person has the power to change their health, and perhaps even their life. Rebekah Eliz leads readers into a deeper understanding of the body's process of vibrant health and simple and effective approaches for healing. Rebekah Eliz is a vibrant speaker, health advocate, and life coach. She lives in New Mexico.

It isn't necessary to embark on a major detox plan to begin living healthier. The key to vibrant health lies in our understanding of biochemical individuality. Applying this knowledge, readers are given the tools they need to jump-start their body's natural healing ability. The simple, three-part "clean/feast/restore" approach to detoxification helps the body repair itself. Together with other supportive practices that include natural nutrition, you can bring your body into balance—and vibrant health. Rebekah Eliz holds a

Master's degree in natural health and is a leading authority in the natural health field. She lives in New Mexico.

CHAPTER 2

Section 1: Nutrition and Diet

Now, let's focus on nutrition and diet. If you want to support and protect brain health and mental acuity, eat plenty of berries, cruciferous vegetables, green leafy vegetables, nuts, and seeds. These are brain-boosters. The best way of aging healthfully, we need to: Decrease our calories by about 25% and focus on healthier foods. Think about creating a diet with fatty fish, avocados, nuts and seeds, olive oil, dark green leafy/fibrous vegetables, and beans/legumes. To support our efforts toward a healthier way of aging, it's good to consider adding in dietary supplements. Here's a short list of what to consider: Omega-3 Fatty Acids (good for our heart and brain), vitamin D, and wound healing nutrients. A diet that contains plenty of fruits and fiber, along with other essential nutrients, is also an important part of keeping our gastrointestinal tract healthy. Our GI system is critical for overall health.

Taking small steps to improve eating and exercise habits, proper vaccinations, routine health care, mental and brain health, and trusting your physician is a good starting point. Nutrition plays an important role in our health, and many aging experts agree that a good diet is one of the first steps in Alzheimer's prevention or delaying its onset. While there is no one-size-fits-all diet, scientists have proven that specific nutrients can boost overall brain health. When it comes to a brain-healthy diet, you need to focus on nutrients like omega-3s, antioxidants, and fiber. These nutrients are extra important as we age, as they can help decrease inflammation and support better overall brain health and more energy. To learn more about ways to guard and maintain good brain health, consider using the information provided by the Alzheimer's Prevention Clinic located in Naples, Florida, and founded by preventive neurologist Dr. Srijon Sen.

2.1. Importance of a Balanced Diet

Breakfast is usually the first metabolic action that the body performs in the day; thus, it is the best time to ingest such foods to activate the body from the early hours. The passion people feel for chocolate is not only due to its exquisite flavor but also to its benefits. Among these benefits is the well-being that chocolate provides. Epidemiological studies show that flavanol-rich foods have beneficial effects on the cardiovascular system. Chocolate also contributes to the increase in the production of epinephrine, dopamine, and serotonergic systems, which amplify the effects of pleasure.

A balanced diet is one of the key aspects in achieving a healthy life because it helps regulate body weight, provides energy to perform physical activities, improves mood, strengthens defenses to fight diseases, and brings a better quality of life. Consuming a varied and balanced diet rich in fruits, vegetables, and whole grains and low in processed foods is essential.

One of the essential tips that can lead to a healthy life is avoiding stress. Try to keep yourself mentally and physically relieved, happy, and free from business stress. You can do this by organizing your environment, exercising, meditation, doing physical activity, deep breathing, and yoga.

Health is one of the key aspects of our life, which we must not ignore at any cost. Healthy living is generally considered to involve balancing the food we eat, work schedules, active and passive life-styles, daily habits, working hours, relaxation, maintaining mental health, and overall physical fitness. We develop bad habits due to stress, improper foods, and exposure to artificial negative energies. In this article, we are going to talk about simple steps that can help you to lead a healthy life.

2.2. Incorporating Whole Foods

Everyone wants to look good every day, right? When our skin looks great, we feel awesome. The skin's care routine—cleansing really well, regularly exfoliating, applying moisturizer and toner, and protecting your skin from the sun—is essential. If you need to begin slowly on your healthy living journey, begin here. Would you like to have clear, glowing skin without having to cover up pimples with a concealer? Examine your plate, eating whole foods is precisely what is required for our bodies to operate optimally. Enjoying an eco-friendly lifestyle while ensuring that nail polish, foundation, sunscreen, and lipstick are natural and safe is the way to go.

Eating a healthy diet, that is wholesome and nutritious, is an-other simple but practical way to look after yourself. Whole foods are a must. In other words, do away with processed food and eat the real thing. Oats instead of granola, ground flax seeds instead of oil, raw honey instead of maple syrup, and cranberry juice mashed from whole cranberries instead of store-bought, sweetened bottled juice. Other tips for healthy living are to get adequate sleep, think positive thoughts, live in a clean environment, and surround yourself with people who love and care for you. Put your happiness first and value who you are.

2.3. Hydration and its Benefits

On most days, regardless of how early my flight is, I end up there waiting for my flight. As in at 3.00 am. I sip water while I gratefully acknowledge the universe that place is there. But I understand that coffee can't always be avoided. So then when I travel, I make sure to drink the same amount of water as coffee—or more! The more water you drink, the less coffee you'll want or need, I promise you. When planning to be stuck on several long flights, always include at least one 1-liter bottle of water in your hand luggage. That much water during a flight needs a planned approach. And not on every possible flight, too. Because the toilets in the air are really not the best place to spend time, in my opinion.

The kids are back at school, and perhaps some sense of routine is beginning to click into place. But you don't have to wait for the end of the year to take up a healthy habit or two. In my book, one of the easiest things to incorporate into your lifestyle is to drink more water—really, it's the simplest way to add years to your life. Your body relies on clean water so much. It benefits your digestion, makes your skin glow, and helps your body flush out toxins. Drinking more water can prevent joint pain and arthritis, it can alleviate constipation, and it can give your brain more energy. Water is the conduit through which our body's electromagnetic information moves, so when you don't drink enough water, you can really come adrift from your regular energy patterns (and negative emotions may find open doors more often!). Because I'm a big supporter of duty-free shopping, my regular route takes me to the Nikau Café past the security at the Wellington airport. This picturesque and very dear establishment sells the best manicure maestros you've ever seen, but it's not the shortbread or the cute cups that attract me.

CHAPTER 3

Section 2: Physical Activity

You also should not begin your exercise regimen with intense levels of exercise or continuous vigorous routines that can cause injuries. Your exercise program should have levels and stages that suit and stimulate your body according to its unique requirements. While remaining consistent, meaningful, and appropriate, effort should be one that constantly challenges your body. It is common for beginners to want to outdo themselves and show their extended capacity. However, this approach can lead to early burnouts and drop-offs in their exercise targets. We would recommend that you take into consideration your resistance to exercise. Select the right pace, stages, and routines suited to gradually build a higher fitness level. By maintaining this pace, physical and emotional benefits are derived, leading to higher motivation and interest for your future exercise levels.

Even when you set specific, achievable, and realistic fitness goals, there is a chance that your initial plans may not remain constant. Due to unexpected changes and circumstances beyond control, your routine may not remain the same. That's normal. Just stay focused. Make adjustments to your fitness goals by setting new ones that fit into your situation.

3.1. Benefits of Regular Exercise

A diet rich in whole foods and low in processed, packaged foods is one of the easiest and most effective ways to nourish your body. When you decide to build a house, would you want to start with already-made building materials that will weather, fade, and crack over time, or would you build a foundation using solid materials that will last and be strong enough to support your house through intense storms and time? Your body has much in common with a house. The food we eat has the power to impact our health positively or negatively. Building your foundation with whole, fresh, organic foods will increase your body's resilience to stand up, survive, and thrive through the tests and challenges of time. Do you want to improve the overall quality of your life? Then build your life with the best materials: whole, real foods.

Regular physical activity can help control your weight, reduce your risk for cardiovascular disease and type 2 diabetes, reduce your risk for some cancers, and strengthen your bones and muscles. Studies also show that physical activity can have strong positive effects on your mental health. People who are physically active are happier and more relaxed than those who are inactive. They find it easier to concentrate, learn, and think more creatively. For many others, the relief of stress, depression, anxiety, or psychological tension is the most important benefit of physical activity. Even 30 minutes a day – five or more days a week – can keep your mind and body in great shape.

3.2. Different Types of Exercise

Flexibility exercises help you feel good with activities done every day. Various methods to stretch the muscles of your legs are important for the ease of physical activity and positioning of the pelvis and lower back. Stretching exercises help stretch and lengthen the muscles; they help keep the muscles and joints flexible and relaxed. In addition, this will contribute to the reduction of work-related injuries and discomfort. The basics of stretching should include the important principles of safety, endurance of individuals, and the ease with which the exercise can be incorporated into a daily routine. A fitness instructor or professional fitness counselor can teach simple stretching techniques based on the needs of each person.

Resistance exercise or strength training is physical activity designed to improve muscular fitness by exercising a specific muscle or muscle group against external resistance, including free-weights, weight machines, or spring-like equipment. The content of strength training can be easily programmed to match the current fitness level of the participant, progresses very nicely, and ensures both adaptation and maintenance of muscular performance. Research has shown this type of exercise lowers the risk of diabetes, stroke, high blood pressure, obesity, and heart disease, and can assist in weight maintenance. Beyond this, resistance training has been shown to increase bone density, which is important for preventing osteoporosis. Muscle mass falls with age, so "use it or lose it" is appropriate, and increased muscle mass actually burns more calories at rest. More muscle and improved body composition from resistance training may also help improve insulin sensitivity and normalize blood glucose levels, which is especially important in type 2 diabetes. Moreover, resistance training increases strength, flexibility, and balance in adults.

3.3. Creating a Fitness Routine

Anaerobic exercises target your muscles, spurring the growth of healthy muscle tissue. While it is important to exercise all of the muscles of your body, it is also necessary to balance the muscles with each other. For example, your lower back should be strengthened in order to follow the strengthening of your abdominal muscles so that your hips and pelvis can be aligned properly. Your bicep and tricep muscles should also be balanced as well as your lower leg and upper leg muscles. When you work out any group of muscles, the other muscles of your body have to become the stabilizers and if there is an imbalance of strength, a clumsy movement may result in injury. Let's not put ourselves in that position.

Here is an overview of a method you can use to build a custom exercise plan. Feel free to make adjustments. After all, this is about improving your life and wellbeing. There are three types of anaerobic exercise you should do weekly to work your entire body: martial arts for your upper body, Hatha yoga for your core, and leg presses for your lower body. Throw in some bicep curls for your arms and some strong buns and legs exercises and you've got your custom, do-it-at-home body workout.

3.4. Importance of Rest and Recovery

I confess that the current fitness goal of pushing and pushing is counterproductive for many people. In this case, my recommendation is to a population that simply cannot abandon this type of exercise. Try different forms of sports, explore yoga, and focus on breathing exercises. Intols should help you reduce stress, and will help you in other ways (described earlier). On the other side of the spectrum, though, did you know that one in three people sleeps too much? According to the rules, 7-9 hours per night is considered normal. Never forget that adequate sleep is the basis of health. But also remember that getting enough sleep is not equivalent to oversleeping! Generally, it is also true that too much rest in our leisure times may not do us good (except in some cases, such as specific diseases or medical conditions). Regular, even biological sleep-wake conditions make it possible to carry out the activities of everyday life without unnecessary difficulty. Consistent rest and relaxation practices combat the harmful effects of persistent overactivation of body functions, such as excessive physical activity or stress.

One of the most important nutrition and health concepts to ingrain into your psyche is the concept of compounding health. This means that the effects of any physical activity that you perform or food that you eat cumulatively have either a positive or adverse effect. Every cookie eaten, every March Madness weekend or Super Bowl can either enhance or impair your health. It is not what we do 10% of the time that defines our health, it is what we do 80-90% of the time. Focus on developing the daily rituals and habits that make you and keep you healthy. Yes, there is more to life than living healthy, but those of us who are healthy certainly have a distinct advantage to living life to its fullest.

CHAPTER 4

Section 3: Mental Well-being

Aerobic exercise is the best way to improve balance, strength, range of movement, flexibility, endurance, and general well-being. Walking is the easiest exercise. Mild exercises like yoga, swimming, brisk walking, and badminton can give substantial exercise and keep oneself active to perform one's work more briskly. Move, move, move, and move will make anyone happy. Mental function was measured through a variety of tests that included memory and speed of thinking. Brisk walking indeed highly increased performance in the 65 participants undergoing the supervised walks when compared with the sedentary control group. Brisk walking also improves physical functions and, in particular, endurance.

A superb vibrancy can only be achieved by serving our mind with the natural state of mental well-being, ensuring long-lasting peace, happiness, and joy. The state of mental well-being and joy can be developed without any underpinning philosophies or belief systems. It is based on the laws of nature and quantum physics. It is simple and easy to acquire. Two hours every day for just two months will surely open a new chapter in your life, granting you 'The Art of Living'. External well-being without internal well-being is not absolutely possible. Thus, as described in the earlier sections, mind management provides necessary balance and makes one lead a balanced and harmonious life.

4.1. Managing Stress Levels

Also, find inspiration, especially when your spirit needs a lift. Your surroundings are influential on how you feel, so ensure your environment is stimulating and energizing. Remember, our body cannot distinguish between a thought and reality. So, if you put a picture up of your favorite literature ideal vacation spot and your mind starts to daydream, let the daydream evoke joy and relief.

It is also important for us to confront our emotions. It is healthier to confront your feelings rather than letting them fester. Learn to confront and release unresolved emotions. Don't hold on to these feelings; find a constructive way to express them, such as keeping a journal or listening to music. Reflecting, meditating, or whatever works best for you.

Here is a tip for you: next time you're feeling agitated, instead of snapping at someone, smile or chuckle. It could change how you feel and alter your mood. Simple steps could include finding the humor, smiling, and counting your blessings. Start having fun, playing, relaxing, and chilling out.

Believe it or not, managing stress levels can also come in the form of laughter because, as the saying goes, laughter is the best medicine. Laughter counters the effects of stress and reduces the stress hormone levels. It also is great for your immune system and takes us away from reality for a brief moment.

4.2. Practicing Mindfulness and Meditation

Meditation increases the stimulation in the attention circuitry and can enhance the ability to direct and focus attention. Over time, continuous practice helps us grow the part of the brain that helps sustain attention and enhances our working memory and other improved cognitive control processes. Meditation gives us endurance and a quiet resolve. Consistent meditation practice does many great things for our brain. Studies using mindfulness techniques have shown significant improvement in mood disturbances, but also a significant increase in brain growth in the areas involved in emotion regulation. Meditation increases the stimulation in the Divided Attention Circuitry, which can improve the ability to divide attention and track multiple things. The calmer state during meditation leads to better thinking and can help us understand why we get so stressed and anxious at work, which can lead to insights into creative problem-solving.

Mindfulness comes to us from an ancient Buddhist tradition and is the cornerstone of the pyramid that allows us to move into higher states of consciousness. Stress is the enemy of good brain health because chronic stress diminishes the number and quality of brain connections and even reduces brain size, which weakens our cognitive strength. We reduce the power of an overactive and overwhelmed mind by slowing down brain wave patterns and thinking less. The great news is that the simple exercise of paying attention to one thing for a time has been shown to reduce the negative effects of stress. There are many ways to pay attention to an object or an activity, from sitting and listening to a piece of music or focusing on a physical object like a candle flame. In paying attention to the current moment, we experience what we are doing as we are doing it. As such, the mind begins to slow down and become more focused. Slowing down brain wave patterns quiets the mental clutter and chatter, stilling the mind and moving us into meditation.

4.3. Building Healthy Relationships

Our relationships are under stress and many problems occur when we neglect the following five important paths to good relationships. Our increasing inability to keep dates and promises. Our inclination to listen superficially, especially when others have a difficulty and want to share something. Our increasing impatience when the other person hesitates to respond; our sense of hurry. When there is less inner satisfaction. If the parents are happy, then the house will be full of happiness and joy and peace. If the mind is calm and full of peace, progress will come. The heart of the house is the parents and not the children. In a true sense, building stability, success, and peace becomes easy when we focus on relationships. Parents must radiate power, prove to be a guiding force for the children and help them solve problems effectively. When the family is strong, anything can be withstood. When there is peace in the heart, the mind becomes very sharp. Peace is a very important aspect of relationships. Helping others is such that my actions and words are in harmony.

The word relationship comes from the Latin words relatus and ionaticus, which together translate as bringing back to a healthy state. A good relationship heals the heart and soul. A good relationship is when others smile when I smile and frown when I frown. A loving relationship means that the other person is more important than I am. We don't fight. Sometimes tension is there, but we overcome it. In a true relationship, we should love, care, share, understand, compromise, respect, accept, adjust, forget mistakes, listen, say sorry if required, and embrace each other daily. Creating harmony in a busy life is an art. Our relationships are a reflection of our state of consciousness.

4.4. Prioritizing Self-Care

Without a prolonged day of rest and recovery, caregivers who routinely place their well-being above their loved one's well-being can feel anxious, deprived, irritable, insecure, and uneasy. Take, for example, the vital role of several thousand unpaid family caregivers who support loved ones with Alzheimer's and related dementias across this region of North Carolina. Their tireless support helps loved ones live in their familiar home environment. Providing this level of round-the-clock or in-home caregiver support often leads to burnout if essential pauses are rarely taken. Those of us who find ourselves surviving (not thriving) or living in chronic stress may benefit from the familiar support of a compassionate person who encourages us to prioritize our daily self-care above all necessary caregiving tasks. If you are someone who easily helps others but finds exemplifying this same caregiving practice impossible, chances are you might just need help finding a path to make it possible for you to significantly improve your own daily self-care. A strong support network (family members, friends, neighbors, or professional caregivers) helps caregivers recharge their many depleted battery cell groups.

In a world in which the demands of work and family seem limitless, self-care often feels selfish or unnecessary. Yet many who eagerly embraced major life changes as teenagers often decide that daily self-care has little practical value. Spouses, children, jobs, aging parents, and academics become priorities. Self-care becomes an afterthought. Their lives become jam-packed with activities and people who need their help. Soon, it can be challenging to find time for personal interests and self-care. This is not unusual behavior. Parents often find themselves managing the lives of their entire family, from children to aging relatives. A 24-hour period lacks enough hours for one family, let alone an extended family. For most family caregivers, their own daily self-care is virtually non-existent. During a busy day, time for a beloved dance class, nature walk, or 20 minutes of yoga with a friend are rare miracles. They may acknowledge their need for self-care as real but also find it virtually impossible to give themselves permission.